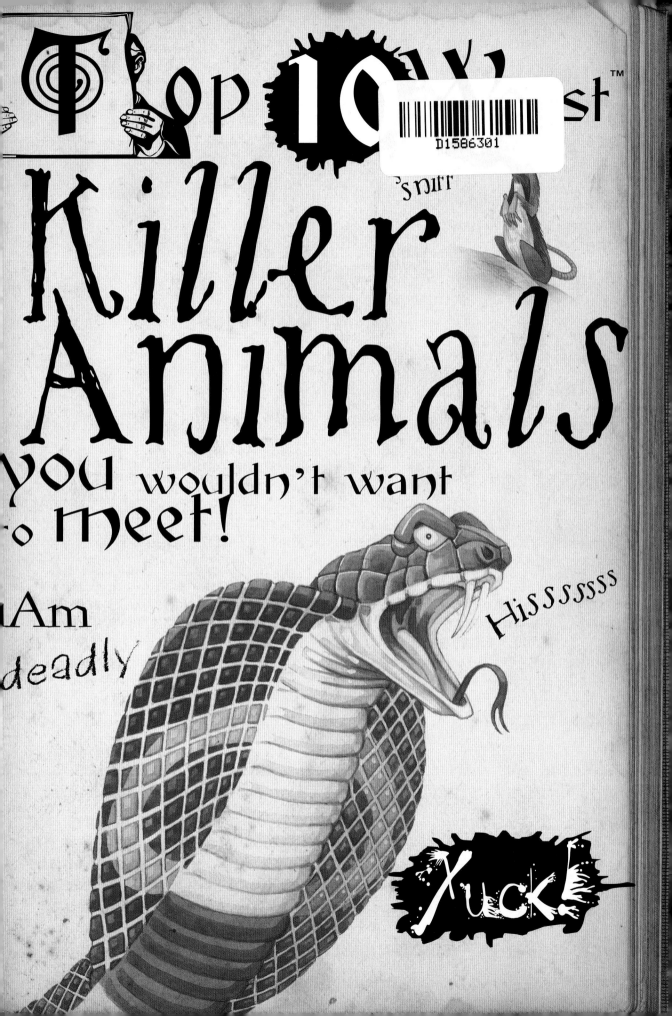

Top 10 Worst

Killer Animals

you wouldn't want to meet!

I Am

deadly

'sniff

Hisssssss

Yuck!

D1586301

Author:
Fiona Macdonald studied history at Cambridge
University, England, and at the University of East
Anglia. She has taught in schools, adult education
and universities, and is the author of numerous
books for children.

Artist:
David Antram was born in Brighton, England, in
1958. He studied at Eastbourne College of Art and
then worked in advertising for fifteen years before
becoming a full-time artist. He has illustrated many
children's non-fiction books.

Series creator:
David Salariya was born in Dundee, Scotland.
He has illustrated a wide range of books and has
created and designed many new series for
publishers in the UK and overseas. In 1989 he
established The Salariya Book Company. He lives
in Brighton with his wife, illustrator Shirley Willis,
and their son Jonathan.

Editor: Tanya Kant

Editorial assistants: Rob Walker, Mark Williams

PAPER FROM
SUSTAINABLE
FORESTS

Published in Great Britain in MMX by
Book House, an imprint of
The Salariya Book Company Ltd
25 Marlborough Place, Brighton BN1 1UB
www.salariya.com
www.book-house.co.uk

HB ISBN-13: 978-1-906714-84-0
PB ISBN-13: 978-1-906714-85-7

S A L A R I Y A

3 5 7 9 8 6 4 2
A CIP catalogue record for this book is available
from the British Library.

Printed and bound in China.
Reprinted in MMXII.

Top **10** Worst™

Killer Animals

you wouldn't want to meet!

Whoosh

snap snap

Yuck!

Illustrated by
David Antram

Created & designed by
David Salariya

Written by
fiona Macdonald

BOOK HOUSE

Top 10 Worst killer animals

Contents

Where in the world?	5
Wild things!	6
Born to kill	8
No. 10: The great white shark	10
No. 9: The Brazilian wandering spider	12
No. 8: The lion	14
No. 7: The saltwater crocodile	16
No. 6: The rat	18
No. 5: The hippopotamus	20
No. 4: The poison-dart frog	22
No. 3: The king cobra	24
No. 2: The Australian box jellyfish	26
No. 1: The mosquito	28
Glossary	30
Index	32

Where in the world?

The ten killer animals in this book live in countries all around the world. Some, such as the rat, are common in many countries, whilst others live only in a few places.

The Brazilian wandering spider lives in Brazil and other South American countries.

Most lions live in Africa, but a few prides still survive in north-west India.

The king cobra is found all over south-east Asia and parts of India.

There are hundreds of millions of rats on Earth – and they live practically everywhere!

Australian box jellyfish are found in the warm seas around Australia and some south Asian countries.

NORTH AMERICA

EUROPE

ASIA

AFRICA

AUSTRALASIA

SOUTH AMERICA

...rogs live in ...opical ...ainforests in ...any different ...arts of the ...orld.

The rivers and riverbanks of central Africa are the hippo's main habitat.

Like rats, mosquitoes are very common throughout the world, but they cause the most deaths in Africa.

Saltwater crocodiles are found around the coasts of northern Australia and south-east Asia.

Great white sharks swim in temperate oceans all over the world, but most attacks on humans occur around Australia.

Wild things!

From the earliest times, the world has been full of animals that kill in all kinds of weird and terrifying ways. Sadly, many of these fascinating creatures are now threatened by the activities of the world's worst killers – human beings!

Chomp Chomp

Hungry dinosaurs!

Giant creatures, with enormous appetites to match, flesh-eating dinosaurs roamed the earth from 254 to 66 million years ago. In Canada, scientists have found coprolites (fossilised faeces) from a *Tyrannosaurus rex* that contain the remains of *Triceratops*, a plant-eating dinosaur 9 m (30 ft) long!

Tyrannosaurus rex

Growl Prowl

Prehistoric predator

Smilodon lived in North and South America from 1.6 million to just 11,000 years ago. These sabre-toothed big cats stabbed their prey in the belly with their two huge fangs (canine teeth). Then, as victims bled to death, they ate them. *Smilodon* usually hunted horses and buffalo, but may just perhaps have killed humans.

Watch out for wolves!

Wolves hunt in packs, using their keen eyesight, excellent sense of smell and sharp hearing to track prey much larger than themselves. In the past, they often killed farm livestock – though, in spite of folk-tales and fairy stories, they very rarely attack humans.

Grrrr...rrrr

Gulp!

Blood lovers ~ vampire bats!

Thumb-sized vampire bats fly by night, using echo-signals to locate their chief prey: insects. But, alone among mammals, they also drink blood, mostly from cattle – but sometimes from humans! They bite a hole in their victim's skin, spit in a chemical that stops clotting, and lap up the blood that pours out. This way, they spread infections, including rabies – a killer disease!

Dragon~worms

In the past, many people in Africa suffered from dracunculiasis – infestation by worms that grew to almost 90 cm (3ft) long. Worm larvae got into the body when people drank dirty water, and hatched there. Adult worms then took a month to chew their way out through living flesh – very, very painfully.

Dragon-worm holes often became infected with deadly diseases.

The Mongolian death worm

For centuries, Mongolian herdsmen warned travellers to look out for the desert death worm. Said to be bright red and hideously ugly, it would spit deadly venom in their faces and sting them with electric rays. Were these stories true or false? No-one knows.

Born to kill

Thousands of animals are killers – but they don't kill for the pleasure of ending a life, or because they wish to do harm. Animals kill for food, to defend their families and territories, or to protect themselves. They kill because they have no choice – they must slaughter to stay alive!

Grrrowl

Polar bears

They swim, float on icebergs, and fluffy toys mimic their wonderful white fur. But polar bears are far from cuddly. They are expert hunter-killers: seals are their favourite prey. Over centuries, they have evolved to live in a harsh environment. But now climate change threatens their survival.

When a tick drinks blood, it swells up to many time its normal size.

Scuttle scuttle

Ticks

These tiny creepy-crawlies need to feed on blood before they can lay eggs, so female ticks lurk in grassland, ready to leap onto passing humans or animals. As they bite and suck, ticks pass dangerous diseases from one victim to another, causing many deaths worldwide.

Ticks are close relatives of spiders. Like them, they have eight legs.

Komodo dragons

Look out! Komodo dragons are 3 m (10 ft) long, run fast and can smell prey from almost 10 km (6 miles) away! The world's largest lizards, they live in Indonesia, where they hunt and eat wild pigs and deer. Scientists used to think that bacteria on Komodo dragons' teeth killed victims; now they have discovered the teeth can inject venom, too.

Komodo dragon

Komodo dragons also eat carrion (dead flesh) and sometimes their own babies!

Squish squash

Watch your step – stonefish!

Stonefish have double protection from predators – and that makes them doubly dangerous. Their camouflage of brownish, knobbly skin hides them on Pacific Ocean reefs, and their backs have a row of spines that inject very nasty venom. If you tread on a stonefish, you might just survive – but you'll suffer excruciating pain.

Vital statistics

To identify animals clearly, scientists arrange them into different groups, under the categories of:

Kingdom e.g. Animals or plants
▼
Phylum e.g. *Chordata* (animals with a spinal cord)
▼
Class e.g. *Mammalia* (mammals)
▼
Order e.g. Primates (apes, monkeys, humans)
▼
Family e.g. *Hominidae* (gorillas, humans)
▼
Genus e.g. *Homo* (prehistoric and modern humans)
▼
Species e.g. *Homo sapiens* (modern humans)

This book tells you which class of creatures each Top 10 Worst killer animal belongs to. The glossary on pages 30–31 tells you a bit more about the different classes of animals.

Remember: Every animal is different! Males and females are also different sizes; usually, but not always, males are bigger. Because of this, the figures for size and weight given in this book are only approximate.

N° 10

The great white shark

Sleek and streamlined, great white sharks glide with ease through the water. They live in temperate seas, from America to New Zealand. Sharks are extraordinary, ancient creatures – fishes without bones! They have tough, rubbery cartilage, instead – a survival from 150 million years ago. Today, thanks to movies and the media, almost everyone is scared of them. Sharks ARE splendid killing machines, but they rarely attack humans.

Vital statistics

Class:	Chondrichthyes (cartilaginous fish)
Diet:	Carnivorous (meat-eating): seals, dolphins and sea-lions
Size:	3.4–6.8 m (10.5–22.3 ft)
Weight:	3000 kg (6600 lb)
Habitat:	Temperate saltwaters
Lifespan:	Up to 100 years
Method of killing:	Biting

Yikes!

Swishhh

Great white sharks can dive 250 m (775 ft) deep. When hunting, they swim, unseen, below their prey, then ambush it by rushing towards the surface and grabbing it!

Be prepared!
Always expect the very worst
How to avoid a shark attack

Don't swim alone. Sharks are less likely to attack groups of swimmers.

Stay calm and quiet in the water. Sharks are curious. Noise and splashing might interest them.

Keep away from fishing boats. They leave a trail of dead fish, blood and guts in the water, which can attract sharks.

Get out of the water if you cut or graze yourself. A shark might detect your blood!

If you brush up against anything rough and scaly in the water, check that you have not been bitten. Cold seas numb limbs, and some shark victims don't realise that they have been injured.

If a shark is sighted, DON'T PANIC but DO leave the water as quickly as you can. Raise the alarm when you are safe on dry land.

Treat all sharks – even small ones – with respect and stay out of their way.

What big teeth you have!

Whoppers of choppers

Sharks use electric fields (forces) in the water to help locate their prey. But sometimes these become confused and sharks eat the wrong thing, by mistake. Unlikely objects, such as car number-plates, musical instruments, and human hands and heads have been found in shark stomachs. None of these – not even human flesh – is suitable shark food. If possible, sharks will try to spit these things out.

Sharks have very sensitive noses; hitting them on the tip can deter an attack.

Sharks can sense blood and locate it from almost a mile away.

Whack!

Sniff

11

No 9

The Brazilian wandering spider

It's silent, it scuttles, and its dull grey-brown colour makes it very hard to spot among dead leaves or in dark corners. Only its mouth-parts are a bright blood red, and, if you can see them clearly, you're far too close for comfort! The Brazilian wandering spider roams town and countryside in many parts of South America, hunting for food. Its bite is deadly – perhaps the worst in the world. And its scientific name, *Phoneutria*, comes from an Ancient Greek word meaning 'murderess'.

Vital statistics

Class: *Arachnida* (spiders)
Diet: Carnivorous: flies, insects, lizards
Size: 10–12 cm (4–5 inches)
Weight: 10 mg (0.0004 oz)
Habitat: Forest floors, boxes, cupboards, car boots
Lifespan: 1–2 years
Method of killing: Venomous bite

You wouldn't want to know this:

Brazilian wandering spider bites can stop your heart beating – for ever – and cause uncontrollable bleeding.

Creep

Be prepared!
Always expect the very worst

Nasty habits

Brazilian wandering spiders:

- are very aggressive and very fast. Unlike most other spiders, who prefer to hide from humans, they will run towards people, jump up on them, and bite them.

- warn victims first. Before they attack, they raise their front legs in the air and rock from side to side.

- can bite repeatedly, every few seconds.

- use their venom to kill prey that is bigger or bulkier than themselves, such as mice and lizards. One bite contains enough venom to kill 225 mice.

- are extremely sensitive to vibrations. Because wandering spiders don't make webs, they monitor tiny movements in their surroundings to tell when possible prey – or an enemy – is approaching.

- eat each other! Like many other spiders, female Brazilian wandering spiders will kill and devour males after mating with them.

Keep calm... don't panic!

Although Brazilian wandering spider venom is extremely poisonous, only 14 people are known to have died from it since 1926. But thousands have been bitten – and many deaths may have gone unrecorded. Sometimes the spider bites 'dry' (without venom) – very scary, but victims survive.

Often, skilled medical treatment saves lives. In 1996, an antivenin (also called anti-venom) to the venom was developed. Since then, no deaths have been reported.

Banana-box killer!

Because it likes dark, sheltered places, the Brazilian wandering spider occasionally stows away inside boxes of fruit destined for overseas supermarkets. Killer spiders have been found in European and North American stores – and have caused panic!

Shriek!

The Brazilian wandering spider's bite is extremely painful.

No 8

The lion

'A pride of lions'. The name says it all! For centuries, lions have been honoured for their courage, strength and beauty. Prides (family groups) of lions used to live in many parts of Africa, Europe and Asia. Today, lions only survive in Africa and north-west India, where they have become great tourist attractions.

Vital statistics

Class: *Mammalia* (mammals)
Diet: Carnivorous: gazelle, buffalo, wildebeest, zebra
Size: 2.4–3.3 m (7.8–10.8 ft)
Weight: 120–225 kg (264–495 lb)
Habitat: Open woodlands, savannah (grassy plains)
Lifespan: 10–15 years
Method of killing: Biting and suffocating

Mythical monster

Lions feature in many ancient myths and legends. For example, Greek hero Heracles wore the beautiful skin of the mighty Nemean Lion. That magic monster could not be killed by human arrows, so Heracles stunned it with his war-club, then strangled it!

14

Be prepared!
Always expect the very worst

Man-eaters?

When most lions meet a human, they run away to hide. But a few lions develop a taste for human flesh and deliberately hunt people. This usually happens when farmers or workers move into lions' hunting territory. In one famous case, at Tsavo, Kenya, in 1898, lions killed 28 railway builders in just one year.

Expert hunters

Lions have spectacular teeth – but they don't kill by snapping or biting. Instead, they grab prey by the throat and hold it tight with their four canine teeth until it stops breathing. Then they use their back teeth like scissors for gnawing, cutting and tearing.

Lions stalk their prey through savannah grasslands – then spring and pounce, to kill!

Killed for fun

In ancient Rome, lions were the star victims of cruel, bloodthirsty contests. They were forced to fight for their lives against gladiators armed with nets and tridents (three-pronged spears). So many lions were shipped to Rome from North Africa that they became extinct there.

Trident

Chomp chomp

No 7

The saltwater crocodile

Descended from dinosaurs, saltwater crocodiles are the largest reptiles living on Earth today – and some of the most dangerous. They live in shallow waters round the coasts of south-east Asia and Australia. Like all reptiles, crocodiles are cold-blooded, and regulate their own body temperature. They bask in the sun to stay warm, or plunge into water to keep cool. They are cunning killers with no enemies, except humans.

Vital statistics

Class: *Reptilia* (reptiles)
Diet: Carnivorous: snakes, turtles, monkeys, buffa
Size: 6–7 m (19.6–22.9 ft)
Weight: 1000–1200 kg (2200–2640 lb)
Habitat: Sea coasts, river estuaries
Lifespan: 70 years
Method of killing: Single snap of the jaws

You wouldn't want to know this:

Crocodiles can swim out to s where they kill sharks – and human swimmers.

Swish swoosh

Each crocodile has around 60 needle-sharp teeth, and extremely powerful jaws. When angry or alarmed, it barks, coughs and hisses.

Crunch Crunch

Be prepared!
Always expect the very worst

Mother love

A female crocodile lays around 40 eggs each year, keeping them warm in a nest of leaves and mud. After 90 days, the babies hatch. When the mother hears their cries, she uncovers the nest and carries them down to the water in her mouth. Then she watches over them until they learn to swim.

Lurking

To catch their prey, crocodiles float half-hidden in the water, waiting for prey to walk or swim by. Then they leap up, grab it and drag it underwater to eat.

Killed for fashion

In the past, crocodiles were hunted and killed so that their skin could be used to make belts and handbags. These were fashionable, costly – and an environmental disaster. Crocodiles became an endangered species. Today, crocodile skins used for fashion items come from captive animals bred on farms, not from wild crocodiles.

It's to die for!

Each crocodile skin has a unique pattern.

Crocodiles' brownish-green camouflage makes them very difficult to spot in muddy waters.

No 6

The rat

They may be small and furry, but rats are far from cute! They spread many deadly infections – and 18 different kinds of intestinal worms! Today, as in the past, crowded, dirty cities are perfect breeding grounds for rats. Feeding on germ-filled rubbish, they spread dangerous bacteria through their faeces and urine. In the countryside, rats kill wild birds and destroy crops, trees and food stores. Rats also carry parasites – creatures that feed off other living things. There are five rats to every person in the world – and their numbers are increasing!

Vital statistics

Class: *Mammalia* (mammals)
Diet: Omnivorous (they eat everything!)
Size: 16–22 cm (6.3–8.66 in) (plus tail 20 cm/8 in)
Weight: 450–520 g (1–1.25lb)
Lifespan: 3 years
Method of killing: Spreading diseas

You wouldn't want to know this:

A female rat can give birth 7 tim a year and can have up to 12 babies at a time. That means that single female rat can have aroun 250 babies in its lifetime!

slurp

Be prepared!
Always expect the very worst

The plague

Arg

The deadliest disease ever spread by rats has been plague. Originating in Asia or North Africa, it killed millions of early Chinese people – and maybe many ancient Egyptians. In the 1340s and 1350s, a plague pandemic spread from Mongolia, killing 75 million people worldwide, including one-third of Europe's population. Plague struck again and again, for example in London in 1665, when 38,000 people died. The last known plague epidemic was in 1994, in Madagascar.

The flea

These microscopic parasites don't just make you itch! As fleas bite to feed on blood, they carry diseases from one living creature to another. In past epidemics, rats infested with fleas spread plague all round the world, as they stowed away on ships or cargo waggons.

The plague doctor

Plague kills most people who catch it – and its symptoms are truly terrible. Victims develop a burning fever plus buboes (huge, painful swellings). Today, plague can be cured, but in the past, all doctors could do was burst buboes with hot metal rods, and prescribe useless herbal remedies. Plague doctors tried (and failed) to protect themselves by wearing leather gloves, wax-coated robes and masks with 'beaks' full of sweet-smelling spices.

squirt!

No 5

The hippopotamus

What a surprise! Plump, waddling, vegetarian hippos are Africa's most dangerous creature! They kill hundreds of people every year, more than lions and rhinos put together. The world's third-largest living land-mammals, hippos' huge size makes them extra-dangerous if they decide to attack. They charge ferociously if their territory is invaded. On land, a charging hippo moves at 32 kph (20 mph) – much faster than any human!

Vital statistics

Class: *Mammalia* (mammals)
Diet: Herbivorous (plant-eating)
Size: 3.5–5 m (11.4–16.4 ft)
Weight: 3000–4500 kg (6600–9900 lb)
Habitat: Rivers, reed beds, grassland
Lifespan: 40 years
Method of killing: Trampling, goring, biting

You wouldn't want to know this:

Hippo teeth are 50 cm (20 in) long. An angry hippo can bite a boat full of people in half!

Male hippos defend their females and territories by challenging intruders. They gape their mouths open, 1.2 m (4 ft) wide, then crash their heads together. They also spray enemies with dung to drive them away.

Gnash

Crash

Be prepared!
Always expect the very worst

Splish Splosh

Graceful giants

On land, hippos are heavy and lumbering, but in the water they move very gracefully. Too dense (solid) to swim, they can close their ears and nostrils, and stay submerged for over 5 minutes. Their webbed toes help them to walk with ease along the river bed.

Ancient enemies

Mummies with badly broken limbs show that many ancient Egyptians were injured by hippos. Egyptians hunted hippos; they also portrayed one of their favourite goddesses, Tawaret, as a pregnant hippo.

Sweating blood?

Long ago, people thought that hippos sweated blood because their skins were covered by a red, sticky liquid. Today we know that this is a natural oil that protects a hippo's skin whenever it is out of the water.

Egret

Grunt!

Egrets

Tall white cattle egrets often follow grazing hippos, or ride on their backs. They find and eat flies, ticks and other small creatures disturbed by the hippos, or crawling on their skin.

21

No 4

The poison-dart frog

Glowing like richly coloured jewels and no bigger than a thumbnail, poison-dart frogs are miniature marvels. Almost 200 different species are found in tropical rainforests all round the world. These mild-mannered creatures kill only for food – ants, mites and flies. But the protective poison on their skin is one of the deadliest substances on Earth.

Ribbit... Ribbit...

Vital statistics

Class: *Amphibia* (amphibians)
Diet: Insectivorous (insect-eating): ants, mites, flies
Size: 2.5–6 cm (1–2.5 in)
Weight: 2.0–6.5 g (0.07–0.23 oz)
Habitat: Tropical rainforests
Lifespan: 4–6 years
Method of killing: Poison

You wouldn't want to know this:

Just two micrograms (0.000002 of a gram) of dart-frog poison is enough to kill a human.

Be prepared!
Always expect the very worst

Do not touch!

• These frogs don't use poison to kill prey or fight other frogs. Instead, they squirt it from special glands in their skin to protect themselves from predators.

• Poison-dart frogs' brilliant colouring warns other creatures not to touch or eat them. Just a single lick can kill! In spite of this, poison frogs are prey to a few snakes and large spiders, which can withstand the deadly poison.

• Some scientists think that the poisons in frogs' skin come from the foods they eat, especially the stinging ants and other insects that crawl on the rainforest floor. If captive frogs are fed non-poisonous foods, they become safe to handle.

Poison darts

For thousands of years, hunters in South America, Australia and Papua New Guinea have coated darts and arrows with frog poison. When these strike prey, the poison paralyses and kills quickly. Cooking poisoned prey makes it safe to eat. The heat destroys the poison.

Caring for the kids

Female frogs lay their eggs on the rainforest floor. Once the eggs have hatched into tadpoles, male frogs carry them on their backs up to tiny pools of water trapped among the plants growing on tall trees. Female frogs feed the tadpoles by laying unfertilised eggs for them to eat.

Croak Croak

No 3

The king cobra

Around 5 million snake-bites are recorded every year – and 125,000 people die from being bitten. Which snake is the deadliest? Experts do not agree – but it's probably the king cobra. It's the biggest venomous snake, the most aggressive, and one of the most feared. Unless they are promptly treated, over half its victims die. And its head can go on biting even after it has been cut off!

Hissssssssss

When threatened, king cobras flatten the skin on their necks to make a 'hood' that makes them look bigger. It's as wide as a man's hand.

Vital statistics

Class: *Reptilia* (reptiles)
Diet: Carnivorous: other snakes
Size: 5.70 m (18.5 ft)
Weight: 20 kg (44 lb)
Habitat: Tropical or sub-tropical forests and streams
Lifespan: 20 years
Method of killing: Injecting venom

You wouldn't want to know this:

A single cobra bite contains enough venom to kill an elephant!

Be prepared!
Always expect the very worst

Keep clear

The most dangerous time to meet a king cobra is during the breeding season (early summer). Female cobras lay eggs in a nest of leaves and guard them fiercely. Male cobras attack anyone who comes near the nest, even accidentally. For the rest of the year, cobras will bite only if they are frightened, trapped or angered.

Open wide!

- King cobras have a very specialised diet – other snakes! They prefer to eat harmless species, but sometimes eat smaller cobras.

- Cobras cannot chew. Instead, their jaws open extra-wide so they can swallow their prey whole – and while it's still alive!

- The cobra's venom paralyses the swallowed creature, and starts to digest it before it reaches the cobra's stomach.

Quick killers

Cobras move very fast, on land and in water. They can also raise up the top third of their body to strike or spit venom at victims! When hunting, they use their forked tongues to flick a prey's scent into their mouths, where it is recognised by a special sensor.

Cobras' excellent eyesight means that they can spot creatures up to 100 m (330 ft) away. At night, they detect their prey's movements by sensing minute changes of temperature.

Hissss

Aargh!

No 2

The Australian box jellyfish

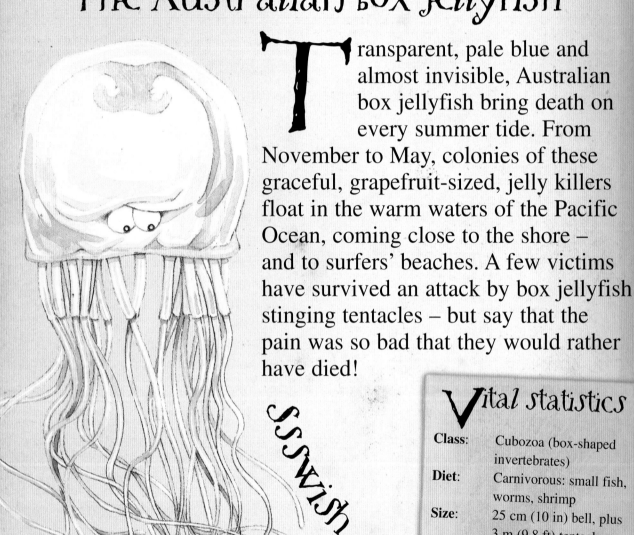

Transparent, pale blue and almost invisible, Australian box jellyfish bring death on every summer tide. From November to May, colonies of these graceful, grapefruit-sized, jelly killers float in the warm waters of the Pacific Ocean, coming close to the shore – and to surfers' beaches. A few victims have survived an attack by box jellyfish stinging tentacles – but say that the pain was so bad that they would rather have died!

Ssswish

Gulp!

Box jellyfish use their tentacles to catch fish

Vital statistics

Class: Cubozoa (box-shaped invertebrates)
Diet: Carnivorous: small fish, worms, shrimp
Size: 25 cm (10 in) bell, plus 3 m (9.8 ft) tentacles
Weight: 2 kg (4.4 lb)
Habitat: Warm Pacific waters
Lifespan: 3–6 months
Method of killing: Injects venom

You wouldn't want to know this:

The box jellyfish makes no warning noise and gives no danger signal. It's a silent, stealthy killer!

Be prepared!
Always expect the very worst

Jet-propelled!

With no arms and legs to carry them, how do box jellyfish move along? By jet propulsion! Box jellyfish shoot through the sea by squeezing their bells (bodies) into a ball, pushing the water out behind them. Travelling this way, they move at around 8 km (5 miles) per hour – as fast as an Olympic swimmer!

One way to guard against a jellyfish attack is to go swimming in a wetsuit – or thick ladies' tights!

Stinging cells

• The long, trailing tentacles of box jellyfish are covered with microscopic nematocysts (stinging cells). Scientists think there are around 3 million of them on every square centimetre of tentacle.

• Each stinging cell contains a barb (spike) as well as deadly venom. If a stinging cell touches a fish – or a human – it explodes, firing its barb and venom into the skin of its prey.

• A box jellyfish sting causes humans instant pain, followed by cramp, vomiting, frothing at the mouth, loss of speech, paralysis – and death. Splashing vinegar onto the sting neutralises the venom, but victims also need rapid treatment with antivenin to fight the poison.

How do jellyfish feed?

As it floats along, the box jellyfish is also busy hunting. Its trailing tentacles are designed to trap small fish or shrimp swimming nearby. Once prey is caught, flaps at the bottom of the jellyfish's bell waft it towards a tube tipped with a four-cornered mouth. The tube sucks up the prey and passes it into the jellyfish's stomach.

No 1

The mosquito

They're almost weightless and incredibly fragile, but *Anopheles* mosquitoes cause more human deaths than any other creature. They spread a dangerous disease called malaria to between 300 and 500 million people every year, mostly in Africa. More than 2 million die. Children, pregnant women, old people and the sick are most at risk.

Vital statistics

Class: *Insecta* (Insects)
Diet: Carnivorous: blood
Size: 0.3–2 cm (0.012–0.78 in)
Weight: 2.5 mg (0.00009 oz)
Habitat: Warm, wet regions, mostly Africa.
Lifespan: 2 weeks – 6 months
Method of killing: Spreading disease

You wouldn't want to know this:

Only females are killers! A microscopic parasite lives in the female mosquito's stomach. When she bites a human and drinks the blood, she injects the parasite into them. It multiplies, and causes malaria.

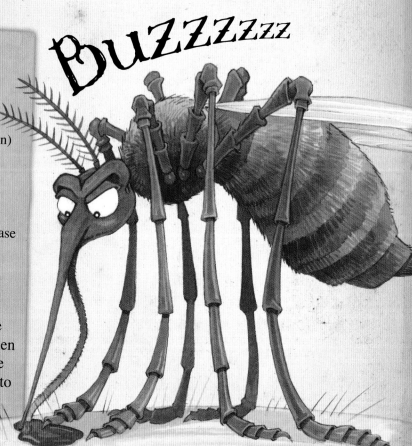

BUZZZZzz

28

slurp

Be prepared!
Always expect the very worst

Please buzz off!

finding a victim

A female mosquito has no nose. But she has sensors that can detect people moving, sweating or breathing out carbon dioxide. Her tiny body also contains chemicals that sense other human smells, and lead her towards them.

How to combat a mosquito attack

Without protection, a person in a mosquito-ridden area can be bitten between 50 and 100 times in one night! The best ways to avoid bites are to:

sleep inside a mosquito net (a tent made of netting).

keep your skin covered.

use anti-insect spray.

coat walls (where mosquitoes rest) with insect-killer.

keep fires burning close by – mosquitos don't like smoke.

Psssst

Life-cycle of a mosquito

After mating and feeding on blood, the female mosquito lays about 200 eggs in shallow water. These hatch into hungry larvae, eating tiny scraps of dead animals and growing all the time. At last, the larvae pupate (wrap themselves in a cocoon). Inside, they transform themselves into adult insects, with wings and six legs.

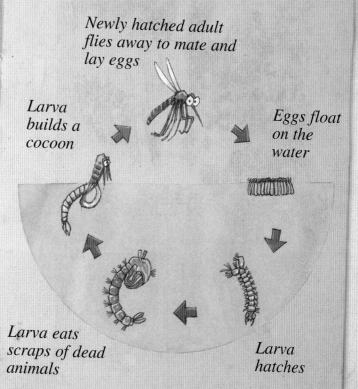

Newly hatched adult flies away to mate and lay eggs

Larva builds a cocoon

Eggs float on the water

Larva eats scraps of dead animals

Larva hatches

Glossary

Amphibian A vertebrate that lives on land or in water and lays eggs.

Antivenin A substance that neutralises venom.

Arachnid An arthropod (animal with a hard outer skeleton) that has a head, a body and eight legs.

Canine tooth A pointed tooth used for tearing food.

Carnivorous Meat-eating.

Cartilaginous fish A fish with a skeleton of bendy tissue (gristle) rather than bone.

Clotting (blood) When blood cells cluster together to form a lump in a vein or a scab on an open wound.

Cold-blooded Having a temperature that varies with the surrounding environment.

Colony A group of creatures that live together all their lives.

Coprolites Fossilised (preserved) faeces.

Cubozoa Box-shaped invertebrates very closely related to jellyfish.

Electric fields Electric forces in nature, that surround us. Some animals use them to locate prey.

Epidemic The fast spread of a disease throughout an area.

Estuary The place where a river flows into the sea.

Faeces Poo.

Herbivorous Eating only plants.

Insect An arthropod (animal with a hard outer skeleton) that has six legs and three body parts.

Insectivorous Eating insects.

Intestinal Belonging to the intestines (lower part of the digestive system in mammals).

Invertebrate An animal without a backbone.

Larva (plural: larvae) An immature animal that will change into another form when it becomes an adult.

Mammal A vertebrate that gives birth to live young and suckles them.

Microscopic So small that it can only be seen through a microscope (a tool that produces enlarged images).

Nematocysts Stinging cells.

Neutralise Work against, make harmless.

Omnivorous Eating all kinds of foods, including plants and meat.

Pandemic The fast spread of a disease across many countries.

Parasite A small creature that feeds from a larger creature and relies on it to stay alive.

Poison A substance that is harmful if eaten, drunk or absorbed through the skin.

Predator A creature that kills others for food.

Prey A creature that is killed for food.

Pupate To become a pupa – a stage in an insect's life cycle when it rests inside a cocoon (protective case).

Reptile A cold-blooded vertebrate that breathes air and has skin covered with scales.

Submerged Under the water.

Sub-tropical Belonging to the regions immediately north and south of the tropics.

Temperate Neither very hot nor very cold.

Tentacles Long, trailing body-parts of sea creatures that often have stings, suckers or hooks.

Tropical Belonging to the tropics – the region between the Tropic of Cancer north of the Equator and the Tropic of Capricorn, south of the equator.

Unfertilised (of eggs) Not fused with sperm, so they will never develop.

Venom A harmful substance delivered by a special part of an animal, such as a hollow fang or sting.

Venomous Using venom to kill or injure.

Vertebrate An animal with a backbone.

Index

A

Africa 7, 14, 15, 19, 20, 28
ancient Egyptians 19, 21
ancient Rome 15
antivenin 13, 27
Asia 5, 14, 16, 19
Australian box jellyfish 5, 26–27

B

Brazilian wandering spider 5, 12–13

C

crocodile *see* saltwater crocodile

D

disease 7, 8, 18, 19, 28
dragon worms 7

E

egret 21
Europe 5, 13, 14, 19

F

flea 19

G

great white shark 10 11

H

hippo 5, 20–21

I

intestinal worms 7, 18

J

jellyfish *see* Australian box jellyfish

K

king cobra 5, 24 25
Komodo dragon 9

L

larvae 7, 29
lion 5, 14–15

M

malaria 28
Mongolian death worm 7
monkey 16, 23
mosquito 5, 28–29

N

nematocysts 27
North America 5, 6, 13

P

parasites 18, 28
plague 18, 19
poison-dart frog 5, 22–23
polar bear 8

R

rainforest 22, 23
rat 18–19

S

saltwater crocodile 5, 16–17
shark 5, 10–11, 16
Smilodon 6
snakes 16, 23, 24–25
South America 5, 6, 12, 23
spider 12–13, 23
stonefish 9

T

tick 8, 21
Tyrannosaurus rex 6

V

vampire bat 7
venom 7, 9, 13, 24, 25, 26, 27
vinegar 27

W

wolf 7